Telling Stories Together

(12 Participation Stories and Patterns for Young Children)

By
Linda Haver

Illustrated by
Liza Sernett

Cover illustration by
Jennifer Ellis

Publishers
T. S. Denison and Company, Inc.
Minneapolis, Minnesota 55431

Standard Book Number: 513-01990-1
Copyright © 1990 by T. S. Denison & Co., Inc.
Minneapolis, Minnesota 55431-2590

CONTENTS

Theme Stories

Holiday-Seasonal Stories

INTRODUCTION

PARTICIPATION STORIES FOR CHILDREN

All young children, active as they are, love to hear stories. These participation stories are especially enjoyed by young children because each story offers them the opportunity to be actively involved in what is taking place.

At the beginning of each story instructions are given for the storyteller. It will be beneficial to the storyteller to be familiar with the story before presenting it to a group of children. Using an expressive voice and knowing where to pause for the children to do their part will add to the children's pleasure.

FLANNEL BOARD STORIES

The children will love being actively involved with the stories in *Telling Stories Together*, but they will also find a flannel board presentation of the stories to be equally enchanting! All the patterns for the stories have been included for you.

So for all those "active" moments in your classroom, let the children have the fun of experiencing being a part of each story by following the directions for using the stories as ***PARTICIPATION STORIES.*** For those moments in your classroom when the children would like some quiet and a visual presentation, use the stories as ***FLANNEL BOARD STORIES.***

Enjoy!

SOUNDS OF THE FARM

This story gives children the opportunity to imitate sounds of a farm. Divide the children into five groups. Each group is assigned to make one of the sounds: cock-a-doodle-do, moo, oink-oink, baa and putt-putt-putt.

Have each group practice their sounds several times. Emphasize to the children that they are to say their sound when you point to their group. In the middle of the story the sounds get mixed up so they must watch you carefully to see when it is their turn.

*Each sound in the story is printed in a **bold, italized** type.*

Farmer Beck was happy being a farmer. He liked the barns, the fences, the fields, the animals, the tractor and the plow, but most of all he loved the sounds of the farm.

Every morning Farmer Beck would wake up to hear the rooster crow, . . . ***cock-a-doodle-do***. Then Farmer Beck would go out to the barn to milk the cows. Each morning the cows would greet him with a loud . . . ***moo***. After the cows were milked and fed, Farmer Beck would take food to the pigpen. The hungry pigs would call. . .***oink, oink*** when they saw him coming.

Farmer Beck's next visit was the sheep pen. He would pat the sheep and listen to them say . . . ***baaa*** while they ate.

After breakfast Farmer Beck would go out and get on his tractor. He would start the tractor and hear the engine go . . . ***putt, putt, putt***. Living on a farm is wonderful, thought Farmer Beck as he plowed the field. I get to hear my favorite sounds all the time. I can hear the rooster crow . . . ***cock-a-doodle-do***, the cows saying . . . ***moo***, the pigs grunting . . . ***oink, oink*** and my sheep calling . . . ***baaa***. Then when I am working in the field I get to hear my tractor going . . . ***putt, putt, putt***.

At lunch time Farmer Beck stopped working and went into the house to eat. After lunch he felt very tired so he decided to take a short nap before he went back to the plowing.

While he was sleeping, Farmer Beck had a very strange dream. He dreamed that it was the next morning and something wierd was happening. Everything was extremely quiet. Farmer Beck looked out his window and saw the rooster sitting on the fence. "What is the matter," Farmer Beck yelled to the rooster, "aren't you going to crow . . . ***cock-a-doodle-do*** this morning?" The rooster shook his head, opened his mouth and out came a loud . . . ***moo***.

Something is wrong thought Farmer Beck as he walked toward the barn. "Good morning cows," said Farmer Beck as he got out the milking machine. "I sure hope you remember how to say . . . ***moo***." The cows looked at him and said . . . ***putt, putt, putt***.

Farmer Beck hurried to the pigpen. I hope I hear the sound . . . ***oink, oink***, he thought to himself. When the pigs saw Farmer Beck coming they grunted . . . ***cock-a-doodle-do***.

The next stop for Farmer Beck was the sheep pen. "Please sheep let me hear you say . . . ***baaa***," he pleaded. The sheep looked at him and said . . . ***oink, oink***.

My favorite sounds are all mixed up, Farmer Brown thought sadly, I guess I will do some plowing while I try to figure out how to fix things. He got on the tractor and started it. Instead of hearing . . . **putt, putt, putt**, the tractor went . . . *baaa*. "Oh no, even my tractor is mixed up," cried Farmer Beck," what am I going to do?"

Just then Farmer Beck woke up. Thank goodness that was just a dream, he thought, I guess I will get back to my plowing.

On the way to the field Farmer Beck saw his rooster sitting on the fence. The rooster greeted him with . . . *cock-a-doodle-do*. Farmer Beck smiled and then walked to the barn. The cows noticed him coming and said . . . *moo*. The pigs were playing in the mud and Farmer Beck heard them grunting . . . *oink, oink*. He stopped to pat the sheep and was happy to hear them say . . . *baaa*. He climbed on the tractor and started the engine. When he heard the engine go . . . *putt, putt, putt* he laughed out loud. This is wonderful, thought Farmer Beck, all my favorite farms sounds are right where they belong.

Sounds of the Farm Patterns

Pig

Rooster

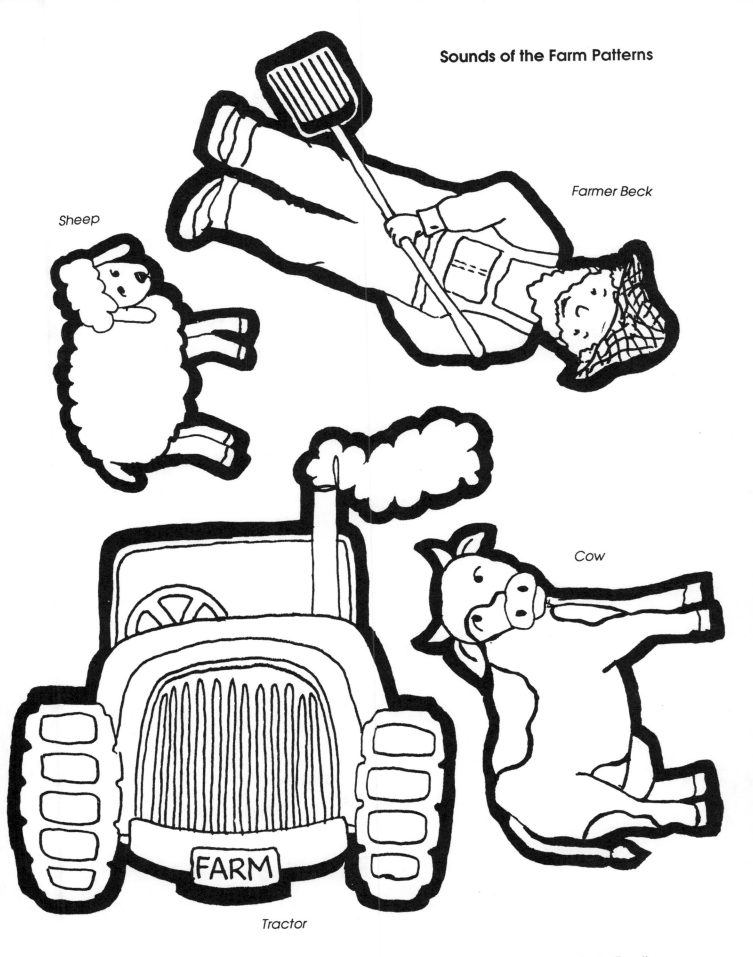

Farmer Beck

Sheep

Cow

Tractor

FARM

MOLLY THE MOUSE

*This is a movement story that deals with opposites such as big-small, outside-inside, fast-slow, etc. The children pretend to be Molly Mouse. All actions that are to be done are printed in a **bold, italized** type. When you are telling the story and you come to a parentheses , do the movement and have the children imitate your actions.*

Everyone should be standing on a carpet square at the beginning of the story. The carpet square serves as Molly's house. If carpet squares are not available you can substitute a hula hoop or a piece of newspaper.

Molly Mouse lived all alone in a tiny house. Molly had never seen the world and was afraid of what might be waiting for her if she stepped outside. I am just a tiny, little mouse **(make yourself very small)** thought Molly, I bet everything in the world is big and tall **(make yourself very big)**. Staying inside my house is probably the best thing to do, Molly said to herself.

At first staying inside seemed like a good idea, but one day Molly realized that she was very lonely. I am tired of being afraid, thought Molly, today I am going to be very brave and go outside.

Molly looked out her door, she looked to the right *(look to the right)*, she looked to the left *(look to the left)* nothing was in sight. Taking a deep breath, brave Molly stepped outside her house *(step off carpet square)*. For a second Molly forgot about being brave and hurried back inside her house *(step back on carpet square)*. I know I can do this, thought Molly, I just need to concentrate on being brave.

In a few minutes Molly was ready and again she stepped outside her house *(step off carpet square)*. This time Molly decided to walk around the house *(walk around carpet square)* just to see what was there. On the ground Molly spotted an ant. "Mr. Ant," said Molly, "you are so small". *(make yourself very small)* "Next to you I look big!" *(make yourself big)* Suddenly Molly felt very brave and was ready to explore the world.

At first Molly walked very slow. *(walk in place slowly)* She looked behind her *(look behind you)*, she looked in front of her *(look in front of you)* since she did not see anything scary she began to walk very fast. *(walk in place very fast)*

Soon Molly came to a big log in the path. On the other side of the log she could hear animal children playing and laughing. I wish I could see what is going on, thought Molly, maybe I can see under the log, *(pretend to look under a log)* but the log was too close to the ground. Maybe I can see over the log *(pretend to look over the log)* Molly said to herself. But she still could not see what was happening. Then Molly had a good idea, she decided she would climb up on the log. *(pretend to climb up)*

Once she was on the log, Molly could see several animal children playing ball. They were so busy with their games they did not notice Molly sitting and watching from the log.

Molly was having so much fun watching the animal children

play that she began to clap her hands very quietly. *(clap hands quietly)* After a while she got so excited that she began to clap her hands very loud. *(clap hands very loud)*

When the animal children heard the clapping they looked and saw Molly sitting on the log. "Come and join us," they yelled, "we need another player!"

Molly did not have to think one second about what she would do. She hopped down off the log *(pretend to hop down)* and hurried to join her new friends.

Molly the Mouse Patterns

Molly's House

Molly

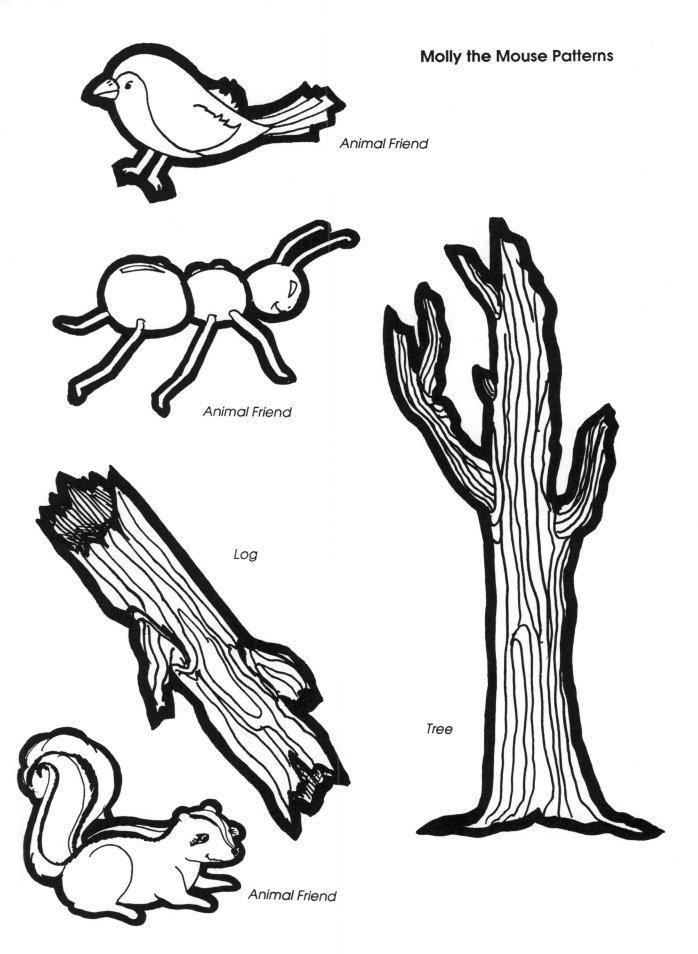

Animal Friend

Animal Friend

Log

Tree

Animal Friend

BILLY BRONTOSAURUS

*When telling this story, pause each time you come to the **bold, italized** "I wish I was different," then point to the children and have them say their line.*
Before you present this story have the children, as a group, practice saying, "I wish I was different."

Mama, Papa and Billy Brontosaurus lived near the edge of a big lake. Mama and Papa were content spending their time searching for leaves and plants to eat and relaxing in the water, but Billy always felt as if something was missing.

One very hot day Billy wandered away from his mother and father. He noticed a grove of trees with lots of inviting shade so he decided to have his lunch. When he got closer he saw a bush that was different than any other bush he had ever seen. Billy leaned down and grabbed a mouthful of tender green leaves from the bush. While he was chewing he began day dreaming about his life. I am tired of being a brontosaurus, thought Billy, other dinosaurs seem to have much more fun than me. Maybe if I had horns like Tom Triceratops I would be happier. Then out loud Billy said ...

"*I wish I was different.*" At that moment something happened. Billy felt a strange sensation over each eye and on his nose. He walked over to a lake and bent down to see his reflection. To his amazement he saw three horns growing out of his head. How wonderful, thought Billy, that bush I was eating from must have been a wishing bush.

Billy could not wait to try out his new horns. He walked a few yards but then realized that his head and neck were extremely tired from holding up those horns. I guess a brontosaurus does not have the right type of head for horns, thought Billy, I need to go back and eat more leaves from the wishing bush so I can ask for something else.

The next thing Billy wished for was flippers like Patti Plesiosaurus. Aloud he said . . . "*I wish I was different*." No sooner were the words out of his mouth when Billy found himself in the middle of the lake. "This is great, " Billy shouted for joy, "I feel just like a sea serpent."

For awhile Billy enjoyed his flippers. He practiced diving and swimming long distances under water. "All this exercise is making me very hungry," said Billy. Then suddenly Billy remembered something very important. Brontosaurus just eat plants and the only thing around was fish. "Fish would make a good lunch for Patti Plesiosaurus," sighed Billy, "but I want to eat some leaves." Luckily Billy remembered that he had saved two leaves from the wishing bush, so he popped them in his mouth. While he was chewing he thought about how nice it would be to have wings like Tammy Pterodactyl. Out loud Billy said . . . "*I wish I was different*."

In a blink of an eye, Billy was sitting on top of a very tall cliff. He could not wait to try out his new wings so he jumped off the cliff and soared over the land. The wind currents carried him safely to the ground. "Boy am I glad that flight is over," groaned Billy, "I think I will leave the flying to Tammy Pterodactyl."

Billy walked back to the wishing bush and took another bite of leaves. This time he thought about how much fun it would be to have big, sharp teeth like Tyrone Tyrannosaurus Rex. So he said... *"I wish I was different."*

As soon as his big, sharp teeth were in Billy started to hurry back so he could show his parents his new look. He had only taken a few steps when he remembered a very important fact about brontosaurus. Tyrone Tyrannosaurus scares brontosaurus, thought Billy. If Mama and Papa see me with these big, sharp teeth they will be afraid. Billy decided he had better take one more mouthful of leaves from the wishing bush so that he could go back to looking like a brontosaurus. Aloud he said . . . *"I wish I was different."*

When he was himself again, Billy slowly trudged home. In the underbrush near the lake he heard a sound. "Who's there?," asked Billy.

"My name is Andy Apatosarus," answered the dinosaur stepping out of the bushes.

"You look just like me!" exclaimed Billy, "but I am a brontosaurus."

"Dinosaurs like us are called Apatosaurus where I used to live," explained Andy.

"All day I have been saying . . .*I wish I was different*," said Billy. "Now I am happy that I look just like an Apatosaurus. We will have lots of fun playing by the lake."

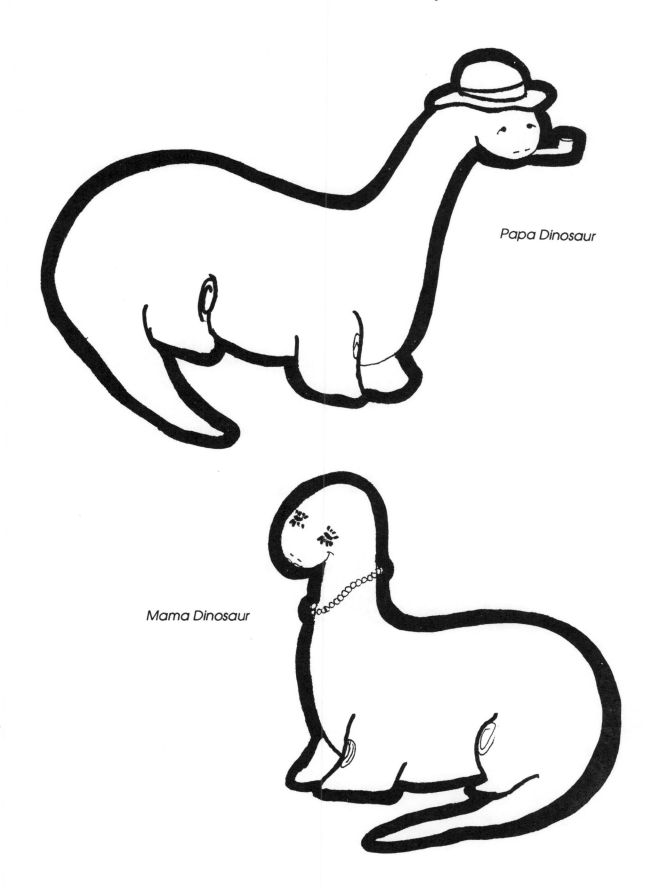

Papa Dinosaur

Mama Dinosaur

21

Wishing Bush

Lake

Billy

Billy Brontosaurus Patterns

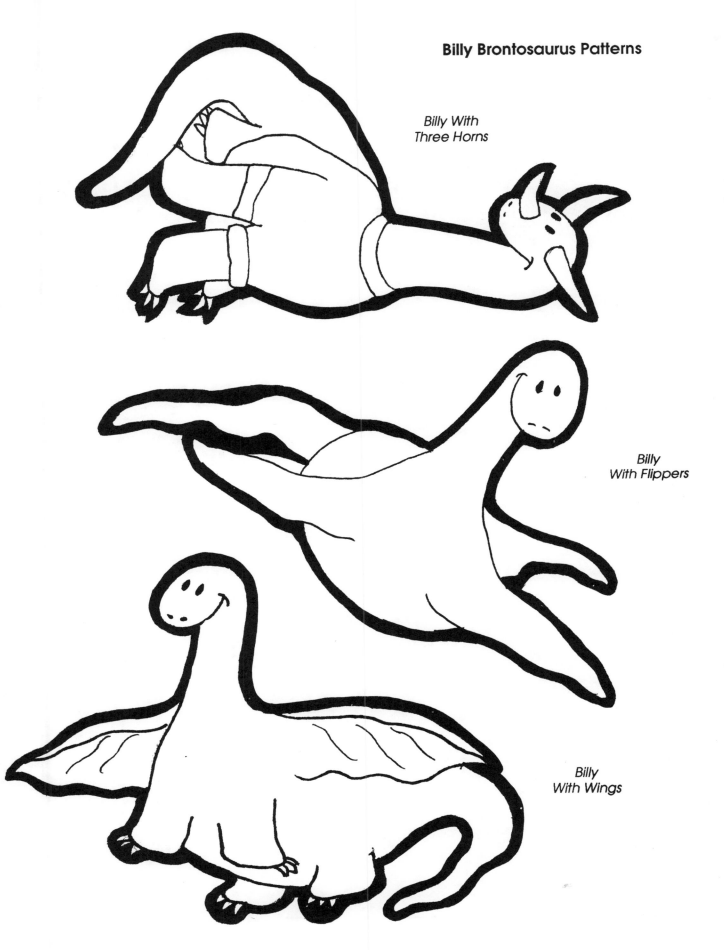

Billy With
Three Horns

Billy
With Flippers

Billy
With Wings

Andy

Billy With Sharp Teeth

MANDY'S MAD DAY

This story deals with emotions. Before you tell the story have the children practice looking mad, happy, scared, proud, sad, surprised and tired. As you practice each emotion have the children think of things that might make them experience that particular emotion.

*Each emotion in the story to be acted out is printed in **bold italized** type. When you come to **bold/italized** word say the emotion with the appropriate expression in your voice and face. Allow the children time to express that emotion before you continue with the story.*

Mandy woke up **mad**. She was not even sure why she was **mad**, she just knew that is how she felt. Maybe it was because yesterday her older brother teased her and called her names, or maybe it was because she forgot to do her homework and her teacher made her stay in at recess. No matter what the reason, Mandy decided that she would be **mad** all day.

On the way to school Mandy met her friend Darlene. Darlene was very **happy** and had some good news. "Guess what," Darlene said to Mandy, "I finally got a puppy." For a minute Mandy was **happy** for Darlene then Mandy remembered that today she was going to be **mad** all day.

When Mandy walked into the classroom before school started, Jack jumped out from behind the door and grabbed her. Mandy was so **scared** that she dropped her books all over the floor. When her heart stopped beating fast, Mandy stopped being **scared** and went back to feeling **mad**.

During language arts, Mandy's teacher announced that she had decided who would be in the school spelling bee from their class. When the teacher announced Mandy's name, Mandy felt very **proud**. Mandy was so busy feeling **proud** that it was lunch time before she remembered to be **mad** again.

On the playground Mandy's friend Sue came over to talk to Mandy and Darlene. "My Dad found out about his new job last night," said Sue. "We will be moving in one week."

Then Mandy felt very **sad**. Sue was her good friend and Mandy would miss her. Mandy felt sad all afternoon, then on the way home from school she remembered about being **mad**.

At home Mandy opened the door and walked into the house. There sitting in the living room were Mandy's grandparents. "Grandmom, Grandpop, what are you doing here?" yelled a **surprised** Mandy.

"We came to stay for awhile," said Grandmom.

After dinner Grandpop asked Mandy what kind of day she had. "I decided this morning that I would feel **mad** all day," Mandy replied. "Then Darlene told me about her new puppy and I was **happy**. Next Jack jumped at me and I felt **scared**. When my teacher said I would be in the spelling bee I was **proud**. Sue told me she was moving and I felt **sad**. When I came home and saw you I was **surprised**. Even though I tried I just could not be **mad** all day."

"Well how do you feel now," asked Grandpop.

"I feel **tired**," answered Mandy. I think I will go to bed.

Mandy's Mad Day Patterns

Darlene

Jack

Mandy's Body

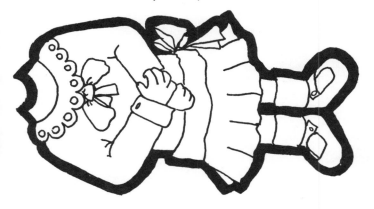

Mad

Mandy's Heads

Scared

Happy

Proud

Tired

Sad

Surprised

Grandmom

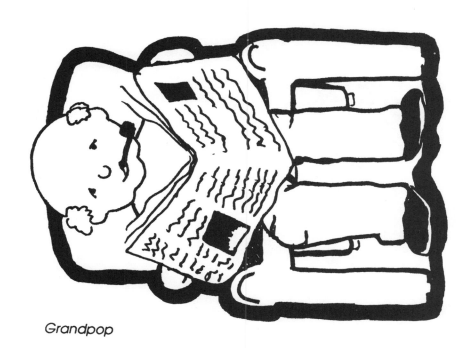

Grandpop

MESSY MITCH

Before you tell this story, have the children, as a group, practice saying, "clean up your mess!"

*When telling the story, pause each time you come to the **bold, italized** sentence "clean up your mess!"*

Mitch was in his room getting ready for school when he heard his sister Nancy yell, **. . . clean up your mess!** Mitch knew Nancy was yelling at him but he did not pay any attention to her. This happened every morning, Nancy would go into the bathroom after Mitch and then yell **. . . clean up your mess!** Mitch did not understand what the big deal was. So he left toothpaste all over the sink, towels all over the floor and the mirror a mess, if it bothered Nancy she could clean it.

On the way back to the kitchen Mitch had to step over several games that he had left on the den floor the night before. Just then he heard his dad yell **. . . clean up your mess!** He knew he had better listen to his dad so quickly he picked up all the game pieces, dumped them into one box and pushed them under the couch.

Mitch was hurring out of the kitchen after breakfast when he heard his mom yell *. . . clean up your mess!* Mitch had left his breakfast dishes on the table so he went back into the kitchen and put his dishes into the sink. I wish everyone would leave me alone, thought Mitch. I am tired of everyone saying *. . . clean up your mess!* I have more important things to do with my time.

Everything was going smoothly in school that day until it was desk check time. Mrs. Adams took one look at Mitch's desk and said *. . . clean up your mess!* Then during free time Mitch made a picture in the art center. He was going back to his seat with his picture when his friend Lee went to the art center and said *. . . clean up your mess!* Mitch could not understand why he was upset. Just because I left scraps of paper and glue all over the table that is no reason to be mad Mitch said to himself, Lee could have cleaned before he made his picture.

That afternoon when Mitch got home from school he had a talk with his mom and dad. Mitch told them that he was tired of everyone saying *. . . clean up your mess!* If my mess does not bother me then it should not bother any one else, Mitch told his parents. His parents smiled and agreed to tell everyone to stop saying *. . . clean up your mess!*

The next morning Mitch got out of bed and got changed for school. He threw his pajamas on the floor and thought, this is great no one will say *. . . clean up your mess!*

This was the best day of my life thought Mitch as he walked home from the bus stop after school. Not once did anyone say...*clean up your mess!*

Everything was wonderful for several days but then Mitch started to notice something. When he went into the bathroom in the morning he could not find his toothbrush or a clean towel and he could barely see in the mirror because it was so dirty.

Downstairs he tripped over the toys he had left in the den and he broke one of his new trucks when he fell. In the kitchen, dishes from several meals were stacked up at his place at the table and there was not much room to eat.

In school Mitch could not find anything in his desk, not even his favorite pencil. When Mitch went to the art center he could not find a place to work on his picture because the table was filled with paper, glue, crayons and paint, I am tired of all this mess thought Mitch. I guess I was better off when everyone was saying *. . . clean up your mess!*

That night Mitch had another talk with his parents. You were right, he told them. Everyone should clean up their mess. I am going to try very hard to be neater, but if I forget just say *. . . clean up your mess!*

Messy Mitch Patterns

Nancy

*Bathroom Sink
With A Mess*

Mitch

MITCH

*Rug With
Games All Over*

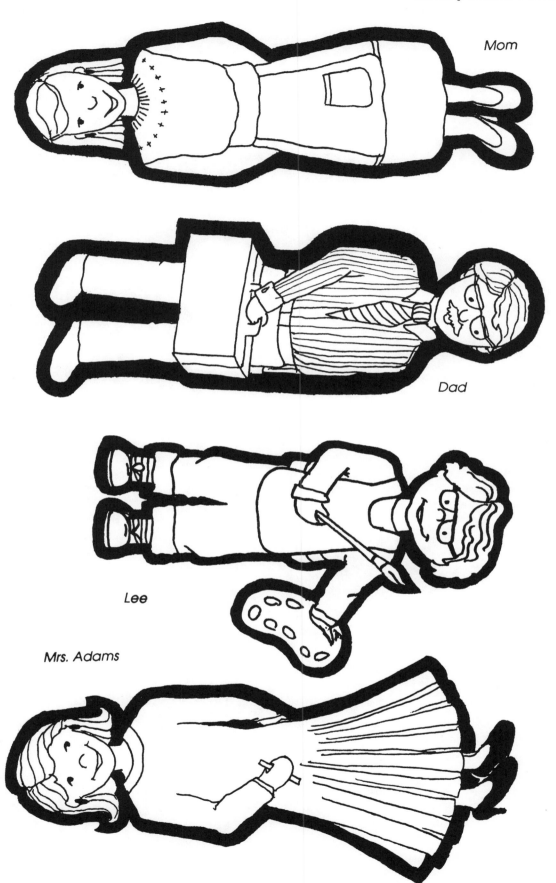

Mom

Dad

Lee

Mrs. Adams

43

Telling Stories Together

*Kitchen Table
With A Mess*

*Art Center
Materials*

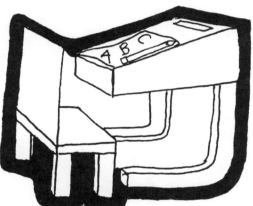

School Desk

BEST FRIENDS

*When telling this story, pause each time you come to **bold, italized** "will you be my friend?," then point to the children and have them say their line.*

Before you present this story have the children, as a group, practice saying, "will you be my friend?"

Benny Bear and Barbara Bear were best friends. They played together every day. When other animal children in the woods would come around and want to play, Benny and Barbara would tell them, "Bears that are best friends play only with each other and no one else."

Everything was fine until Barbara Bear got the flu and had to spend a whole week in bed. The first day Barbara was sick, Benny spent all day alone, playing with his toys. By the second day Benny was lonely and he wished he had another friend to play with.

Benny decided to go out and look for someone to be his friend.

Benny had not walked very far when he met Randy Raccoon. Benny smiled at Randy and said . . ."**will you be my friend?**" but Randy Raccoon kept right on walking.

A little farther down the road Benny saw Sandy Squirrel. Benny smiled at Sandy and said . . . "**will you be my friend?**" but Sandy just smiled back and shook her head.

Soon Benny ran into Danny Deer. Benny smiled at Danny and said . . . "**will you be my friend?**" Danny Deer just hurried by and went on down the road.

Ricky Rabbit came hopping along. When he saw Ricky, Benny smiled and said . . . "**will you be my friend?**" but Ricky kept right on hopping.

Next Benny met Gary Groundhog. Benny smiled at Gary and said . . ."**will you be my friend?**" Gary Groundhog looked at the ground and kept right on walking.

By this time Benny was tired of saying . . . "**will you be my friend?**" so he turned around and sadly started walking back home. As he walked, Benny started thinking about Randy Raccoon, Sandy Squirrel, Danny Deer, Ricky Rabbit and Gary Groundhog. At first Benny was mad that none of the animal children would be his friend, but then he remembered how he and Barbara would never let any of the animal children play with them. I guess I got just what I deserved thought Benny.

Just then Benny heard someone say . . . . "**will you be my friend?**" He turned around and saw Randy Raccoon, Sandy Squirrel, Danny Deer, Ricky Rabbit and Gary Groundhog all standing by a tree. They all looked at Benny and said again. .. "**will you be my friend?**" Benny was so happy he shouted "yes!, and when Barbara gets well we can all be best friends."

Barbara Bear

Benny Bear

Sandy Squirrel

Randy Raccoon

Ricky Rabbit

Danny Deer

Gary Groundhog

THE NEW FRIENDS BAND

For this story divide the children into three groups. The horn group shoud practice saying toot-toot, the drum group should practice saying dum-dum and the xylophone group sould practice saying ding-ding. Pause when you come to . . . and the **bold, italized** type, point to the appropriate group so they can do their sound. At times two or more instruments play simultaneously, then the children in those groups should do their sounds at the same time.

Todd had just moved to a new city and he was very lonely. At his old house he had a lot of friends to play with right in his neighborhood, but in this new apartment building he did not know anyone. It was a few weeks until school started so Todd spent most of his time playing his horn.

Todd loved the sound of his horn . . . ***toot-toot***. He would play it every day. His mom could hear him practicing in the moring . . . ***toot-toot***. Right after lunch he would play a song . . . ***toot-toot***. When his dad came home, Todd was practicing again . . . ***toot-toot***.

One day Todd's mother walked into his room while he was playing his horn . . . ***toot-toot***. She told Todd that she loved hearing his horn . . . ***toot-toot***, but it was too nice a day to be inside. So Todd decided to go to the playground.

When Todd was walking down the stairs he heard a noise coming from the recreation room . . . ***dum-dum***. That sounds like a drum, thought Todd. As he got closer the noise became louder . . . ***dum-dum***. Todd opened the recreation room door and there he saw a boy about his age playing a drum . . . ***dum-dum***. Todd went over to the boy and introduced himself. Todd learned that the boy's name was Brian. After talking to Brian for a few minutes, Todd ran back to his apartment to get his horn.

As soon as Todd got back with his horn, the two boys started playing together . . . ***toot-toot, dum-dum***. It sounded wonderful! They played their instruments for an hour . . . ***toot-toot, dum-dum***. It was the best time Todd had since he moved to the city, he was so happy to have a friend. They decided to meet every day at the same time and start a band.

The next morning Todd went for a walk with his mom and told her all about his new friend Brian. Todd told her how great it was to have a friend that liked music as much as he did.

After lunch Todd grabbed his horn and hurried down the stairs to the recreation room. As he neared the door he could already hear Brian playing his drum . . .***dum-dum***. Todd sat down and began playing his horn . . . ***toot-toot***. They played together for awhile . . . ***toot-toot, dum-dum***, then decided to go to the playground. Just as they were leaving a girl carrying a xylophone came into the recreation room. She told them that her name was Nancy and she had just moved into the apartment building. She played her xylophone for them . . . ***ding-ding***, then asked if she could join their band. Todd and Brian were happy to have another friend in their band so they all started playing their instruments ... ***toot-toot, dum-dum, ding-ding***. It sounded fantastic! They played all afternoon . . . ***toot-toot, dum-dum, ding-ding***. They decided they should have a name for their band so they became known as "The New Friends Band."

From then on everyone in the apartment building enjoyed hearing The New Friends Band practicing every afternoon . . . *toot-toot, dum-dum, ding-ding.*

The New Friends Band Patterns

Horn

Todd

Mom

Dad

Nancy Holding
Her Xylophone

Brian Sitting
Playing His Drum

COLORS OF FALL

*When you are telling this story, pause each time you come to an **bold, italized** color word. The children are to identify the appropriate color by holding up a crayon or piece of paper of that color. Each child should have the colors red, orange, brown, green and yellow.*

For a variation, instead of holding up the appropriate color, you might try having the child raise their hand each time you mention a color they are wearing.

Kate and Barry both loved fall, it was their favorite season of the year. One day their teacher asked them to write a report about why they felt fall was the best season. "This will be an easy report," Barry told Kate, "of course we like fall because of football and cooler weather."

"Wait one minute," said Kate, "the reason we like fall is because of soccer and the start of a new school year."

Barry thought a second then said, "No that is not the reason we like fall. The best thing about fall are all the pretty colors of the changing leaves."

"You are right," Kate agreed, "the colors are the very best part of fall, and **red** is the prettiest fall color. **Red** reminds me of fire trucks, candy apples and Valentines."

"I think **orange** is the nicest color," Barry replied. **Orange** is the color of pumpkins, squash and goldfish."

"**Orange** is nice," said Kate, "but how about **brown**?" **Brown** makes me think of bears, chocolate cake, and root beer."

"**Green**, we forgot about **green**," exclaimed Barry. "**Green** is the color of grass, frogs and celery."

"Another color that I really like is **yellow**," said Kate. "**Yellow** always makes me think of sunshine, bananas, and corn."

"I have an idea for our report. We should gather some pretty fall leaves, press them between waxed paper and label what kind of tree they grew on," explained Barry.

On the way home from school Barry and Kate started looking for different colored leaves. Under the maple tree on the playground, they found several perfect **red** leaves. Next to the maple tree was an oak tree, there they found beautiful **yellow** leaves.

When they were done collecting leaves on the playground Kate and Barry started down the street. In Kate's front yard they picked up a couple **orange** leaves. They went into the back yard and found more **red** leaves. "Let's get a snack then go to your house to look for leaves," Kate told Barry.

At Barry's house they discovered a tree with **green** leaves. They picked up some pretty ones, then went searching for **brown** leaves. While they were looking they found more **orange** leaves. "I think we have enough leaves," said Barry. "Why don't we get started on our report?"

"Great," replied Kate, "we have leaves that are **red**, **green**, **orange**, **yellow** and **brown**, all the colors of fall."

Colors of Fall Patterns

Barry

Kate

Red Maple Leaf

Orange Maple Leaf

Brown Oak Leaf

Green Oak Leaf

Yellow Oak Leaf

GORDON THE GHOST

For this story, divide the children into three groups. The wind group should howl, the black cats meow and the witches cackle. Allow time for each group to practice their part.

When you are telling the story, pause each time you come to a **bold, italized** instruction and point to the appropriate group and give them time to do their part.

The wind **howled** . . ., the black cats **meowed** . . ., the witches **cackled** . . ., it was Halloween. But Gordon the ghost did not feel much like celebrating. All of the other ghosts were busy practicing their Halloween tricks, but Gordon was feeling very sad and very sorry for himself.

"I wish I was not a Halloween ghost," said Gordon, "everything else about Halloween is so scary. The wind **howling** . . ., the black cats **meowing** . . ., the witches **cackling** . . .. But I am just a little ghost and I am not at all important to Halloween. Maybe I could pretend to be something else this Halloween, I will go see Wise Old Owl, maybe he can help me."

As Gordon walked along to see Wise Old Owl it was getting dark. He could hear the wind **howling** . . ., the black cats **meowing** . . ., and the witches **cackling** . . ., he knew the time for Halloween tricking was getting close.

"Wise Old Owl," said Gordon when he came to the big oak tree where the owl lived, "please help me!"

"What is the problem?" said Wise Old Owl.

"I want to be something special this Halloween. The wind **howls** . . ., the black cats **meow** . . ., the witches **cackle** . . ., but no one needs a little ghost like me at Halloween."

"I have an idea," said Wise Old Owl, "why don't you go visit the wind that **howls** . . ., the black cats **meow** . . ., the witches that **cackle** . . ., and see if you can join them this Halloween."

So Gordon the ghost was off to visit the wind that **howled**. When he came to where the wind lived, Gordon started **howling** . . ., and yelling, "listen to me wind, can I howl with you this Halloween?"

"Sure," said the wind, "Halloween can always use more howling, come join us."

Well, Gordon **howled** . . . down on street, he **howled** . . . up another street, he **howled** . . . all over town. But he discovered that he really did not like howling. So Gordon the ghost said good-by to the wind and went off to visit the black cats.

When he came to where the black cats lived, Gordon started **meowing** . . . and shouting, "black cats I want to be like you this Halloween, can I meow with you?"

"Of course you can," answered the black cats.

Gordon went *meowing* . . ., down one street, meowing up another street, *meowing* . . . all over town. But he found that he did not like meowing either, so Gordon the ghost said good-by to the black cats and went off to visit the witches.

When he came to the place where the witches lived, Gordon *cackled* . . . as loud as he could. "Listen to me witches, I want to cackle with you this Halloween. Can I join you?"

The witches said, "we would love to have the company."

So Gordon *cackled* . . . down one street, he *cackled* . . . up another street, he *cackled* . . . all over town. But he learned that he did not like cackling, so Gordon the ghost said good-by to the witches and started on his way home.

As he walked along, Gordon was still feeling very sad and very sorry for himself. I tried being the wind that *howls* . . . . I tried being a black cat that *meows* . . .. I even tried being a witch that *cackles* . . ., but I am still not happy.

As Gordon walked farther he saw a little boy named Kevin going down the street with his mother. As Gordon got closer he could hear Kevin say to his mother, "Mom, I am so sad, this has been a terrible Halloween. We heard the wind *howling* . . .. We heard the black cats *meowing* . . .. We heard the witches *cackling* . . ., but it just does not seem like Halloween because not one ghost played a Halloween trick on us."

When he heard what Kevin said, Gordon whished down over Kevin and his mother and knocked the hat right off Kevin's head.

Kevin shouted, "A ghost, a real ghost, it was a wonderful Halloween after all."

Well that made Gordon the ghost feel very important and very happy. Never again did Gordon want to be the wind *howling*. . ., the black cats *meowing* . . ., or the witches *cackling* . . .. Gordon was happy just being himself!

Kevin

Gordon

Howling Wind

Black Cats Meowing

Witches Cackling

Wise Old Owl In Tree

Kevin's Mom

LUCY LEPRECHAUN

*In this story the children are instructed to move around in a circle while either walking, hopping, tiptoeing, jogging or skating. When you say a **bold, italized** movement word the children are to go around the circle doing the appropriate action. When you say stop they should "freeze".*

This story also deals with selfishness. You might want to discuss the meaning of selfish before you tell the story.

In a dark green forest in Ireland lived a leprechaun named Lucy. Lucy did not have many leprechaun friends because she was selfish. She never wanted to share anything so no one wanted to play with her. Lucy pretended that she did not care, she would make up games and play them all by herself.

One day Lucy saw a bright coin lying on the ground. Some leprechaun must have dropped a piece of gold from his pot, thought Lucy. She bent down to pick up the coin. When the coin was in her hand something magical happened. Faster than the blink of an eye she was in a beautiful open field. Lucy had never been out of the forest. Leprechauns always stayed in the forest where there were lots of trees and rocks to hid behind. At first Lucy was frightened but in a while she realized this wonderful place was safe for leprechauns.

Since Lucy was not used to wide open places, she began **walking** around in a big circle. I know a great game I can play here, thought Lucy. I will go around in a big circle, moving all different ways. Then when I yell "stop," I will freeze.

First Lucy tried **walking** around the circle. When she had gone about half way around she yelled, "**stop**."

Next Lucy **hopped on one foot**. She could not go as fast that way so she said, "stop". That tired me out, thought Lucy, this time I will try tiptoeing. This is easy, I can go all around the circle this way. Soon Lucy got bored with tiptoeing and whispered "**stop**."

Lucy decided to try **jogging**. This is more fun, Lucy said to herself, I will keep jogging. She jogged until she could not take another step, then she yelled "**stop**."

Now I will pretend to **skate**, thought Lucy. She liked skating and kept going round and round the circle. I bet I look just like an olympic skater, but I think I had better say, "**stop**."

Lucy was getting tired of the game so she picked up the magic coin and quick as a blink she was back in her forest.

Lucy never told any of the other leprechauns about the magic coin. Every day she would use the coin to go to the field. While she was there she would play her circle game.

After about a week Lucy tired of her game. This game would be much more fun if if I did not have to play alone, thought Lucy, maybe I should invite some other leprechauns to come to the magic field.

Lucy found the other leprechauns behind the big oak tree. Some of them were picking shamrocks, others were counting the coins in their pots of gold. The leprechauns were surprised when Lucy invited them to the magic field she had discovered.

Lucy and the other leprechauns all held hands and Lucy picked up the magic coin. Quick as a blink they were all transported to a wide open field. Lucy explained the rules of her game and they began to play.

"**Walk**," said Lucy. The leprechauns walked around the circle several times, then Lucy yelled, "**stop**." Next Lucy told them to **hop on one foot**. Leprechauns are not good at hopping but they all had fun trying to do their best. "**Stop**," yelled Lucy.

"**Tiptoe**," whispered Lucy. The leprechauns quietly tiptoed around and around the circle. Lucy yelled, "**stop**."

"The next thing we are going to do is **jog.**" They all liked jogging so Lucy let them jog around the circle two times before she yelled, "**stop**."

"The last thing we are going to do is **"skate."** The leprechauns had never skated before but they had a great time skating around the circle until Lucy yelled, "**stop**."

"This was such a great day!" said Lucy. "Will you come back with me tomorrow and play more games?" The leprechauns all answered "yes." From that day on Lucy was never selfish again because she had learned that sharing was fun.

Coin

Tree

Lucy

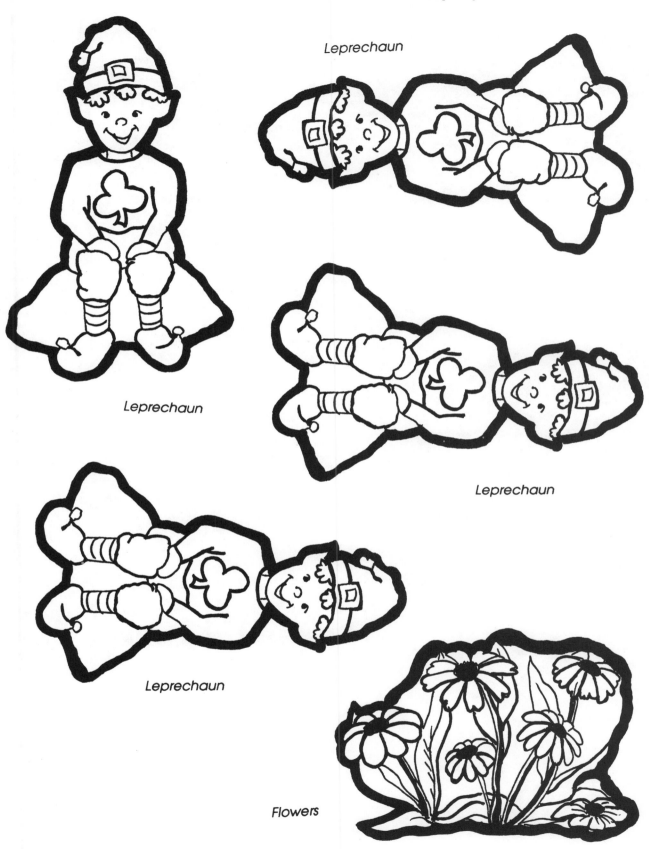

Leprechaun

Leprechaun

Leprechaun

Leprechaun

Leprechaun

Flowers

MICKEY'S VALENTINE GIFT

In this story the children pantomime every day actions such as brushing their teeth and making their bed.
   *The actions that should be pantomimed are in a **bold, italized** type. Pantomime each action and have the children imitate your movement.*

Mickey ***hopped*** out of bed then ***walked*** into the bathroom. He looked into the mirror and frowned. Today is Valentines' Day and I can not think of anything to do to show Mom and Dad how much I love them, thought Mickey. While in the bathroom, he ***brushed*** his teeth and ***washed*** his face. Slowly he went back to his bedroom, still trying to think of something special to do for his parents.

In his room, Mickey ***got dressed*** and ***made his bed***. Then Mickey ***picked up his toys*** and ***put them into his toy box***. "Mom and Dad love me and do so much for me, I sure wish I could think of something to do for them," sighed Mickey as ***he walked down the stairs one step at a time***.

When he went into the kitchen Mickey said good morning and sat down at the table. He saw that his mom was busy cooking breakfast so when his baby sister dropped her spoon *he picked it up* and handed it to her. After he ate, Mickey *carried his dishes over to the sink*. Mickey remembered that today was garbage pick-up so he got a garbage bag and started *emptying all the trash cans in the house into the bag*. When he was done he *carried the garbage bag outside and put it on the curb*. All the while Mickey was trying to think of a way to show his love to his parents.

Back in the house, Mickey found his parents and decided to tell them his problem, "Mom and Dad, all morning I have been trying to think of a way to show you how much I love you but I just can not come up with any ideas."

His parents smiled, gave him a big hug and said, "Mickey, you have been showing us your love all morning. You *brushed your teeth, washed your face, made your bed and picked up your toys* without even being asked. Then when you came downstairs you were such a good helper. You *picked up your sister's spoon, carried your dishes to the sink and collected the garbage*."

Mickey smiled, hugged his parents and said, "Happy Valentine's Day!"

Bathroom Sink

Micky

Mickey's Bed

Staircase

Toy Box

Trash Can

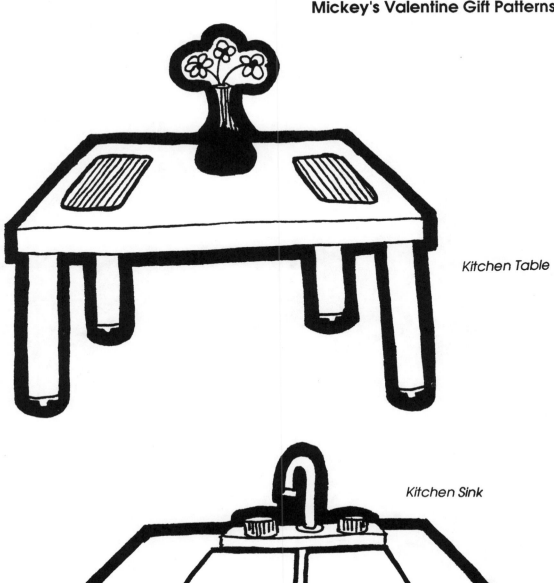

Kitchen Table

Kitchen Sink

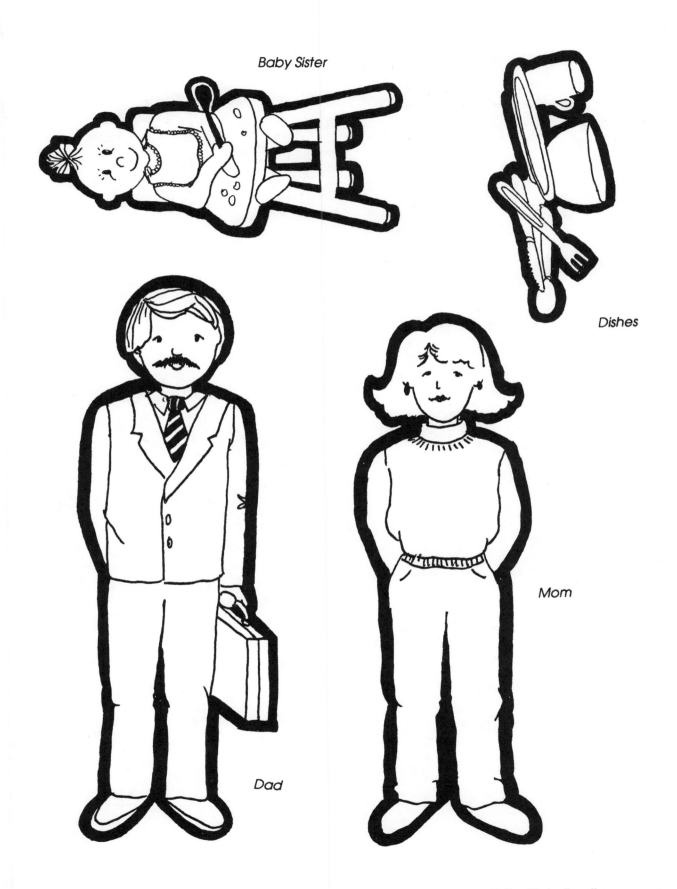

Baby Sister

Dishes

Mom

Dad

SIGNS OF SPRING

*In this story the children will be acting out signs of spring. When you come to . . . pause then allow the children to act out the **bold, italized** phrases.*

After the story you might want to let the children think of other signs of spring that Jimmy and Kimmy could learn about on their next trip out of the barnyard.

Mother Sheep gently nudged her twin baby lambs, Jimmy and Kimmy. "Wake up," whispered Mother Sheep, "This is your first spring, it is time to get up and see the world. Today you may go out on your own to see all the wonderful signs of spring. I will be here in the barnyard if you need me."

Jimmy and Kimmy were so excited they began to prance all around the barnyard. "Let's go," squealed Kimmy, "I can not wait to see spring."

As they walked toward the meadow, Jimmy suddenly became very sad. "Kimmy," said Jimmy, "We have never seen spring, how will we know what to look for while were are exploring?"

Kimmy thought for a moment then replied, "I know, let's ask some of the other animals in our neighborhood if they have seen spring. Maybe they can tell us how it looks.

Just then Freddy Frog came hopping up from the pond. Jimmy and Kimmy hurried over to Freddy and asked him if he could tell them a sign of spring.

"Sure I can tell you a sign of spring," said Freddy, "spring is when . . . the **warm sun shines down and all the frogs and turtles crawl out from the mud after their long winter nap**."

"Thank you, Freddy," said Jimmy. "Come on Kimmy we will see what else we can discover about spring."

The lamb twins had gone just a short distance when they met Samantha Skunk. "Samantha," yelled Kimmy, "How do you tell when it is spring?"

"That is easy," answered Samantha. "I can always tell it is spring when . . . **the warm rain comes down and the flowers in the meadow burst into bloom**."

After thanking Samantha for her help, the twins got back to exploring. Soon they came to a bee hive where a swarm of busy bees were at work.

"Hello, bees," shouted Jimmy, "Can you tell us a sign of spring?"

"Certainly," replied Bobby Bee, "A sure sign of spring is when you see . . . **the bees flying in and out of the flowers gathering nectar and pollen**."

"Thank you for your help, Bobby," said Jimmy.

"All this exploring is making me tired," sighed Kimmy. "How about if we find one more sign of spring, then go back for our nap."

As they walked back toward the barnyard they met Harriet Hen. The two lamb twins ran right up to Harriet and asked, "Can you tell us a sign of spring?"

"Why, of course," answered Harriet. "I can always tell it is spring when . . . **my bird friends fly back from the south and spend their time building nests.**"

"You have been a big help," the lambs told Harriet, "Thank you very much."

Mother Sheep spotted her babies and went over to ask them if they had found any signs of spring.

Excitedly, Jimmy and Kimmy told their mother all about their adventure into the world. "We learned that in spring . . . **the warm sun shines down and the frogs and turtles crawl out of the mud**. We also found out that . . . **the warm rain comes down and helps to make the flowers burst into bloom**. Another sign of spring is . . . **the bees fly all around and gather nectar and pollen from the flowers**. Also you can tell it is spring when . . . **the birds fly back from the south and start to build their nests.**"

"That is wonderful," said mother sheep, "You have learned so much. Now it is time for your nap. Tomorrow you can go exploring for more signs of spring."

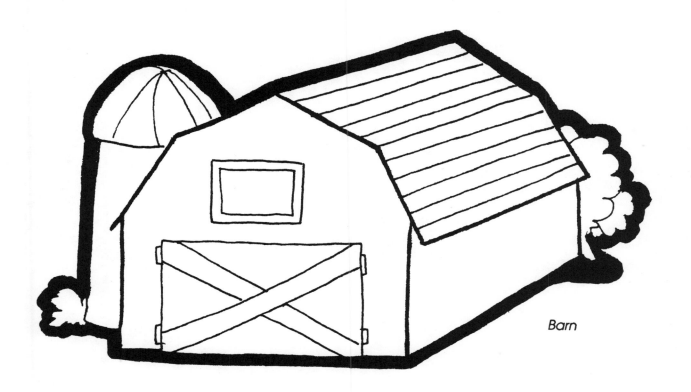

Barn

Mother Sheep

Jimmy

Kimmy

Sun

Freddy Frog

Cloud
With Raindrops

Samantha Skunk

Pond With
Frogs & Turtles

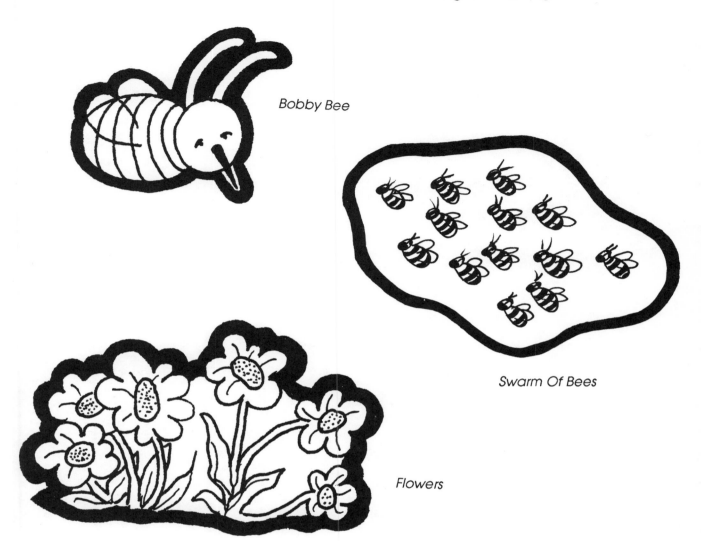

Bobby Bee

Swarm Of Bees

Flowers

Flowers

105

Telling Stories Together

Harriet Hen

Nest

Nest

Small Birds

107

Telling Stories Together

TEACHER'S NOTES

TEACHER'S NOTES

TEACHER'S NOTES

TEACHER'S NOTES

TEACHER'S NOTES